T0284441

Enduring Wisdom

Enduring Wisdom

Words of Hope and Inspiration by
Her Majesty Queen Elizabeth II

First published in Great Britain in 2024

SPCK
SPCK Group
Studio 101
The Record Hall
16–16A Baldwin's Gardens
London EC1N 7RJ
www.spckpublishing.co.uk

The Christmas broadcasts of Her late Majesty Queen Elizabeth II are
available in full at: https://www.royal.uk/christmas-broadcast-1956

British Library Cataloguing-in-Publication Data
A catalogue record for this book is available from the British Library

ISBN 978–0–281–09037–2
eBook ISBN 978–0–281–09038–9

1 3 5 7 9 10 8 6 4 2

Typeset by Fakenham Prepress Solutions, Fakenham, Norfolk NR21 8NL
First printed in Turkey by Mega Print

eBook by Fakenham Prepress Solutions, Fakenham, Norfolk NR21 8NL

Produced on paper from sustainable sources

Contents

PART 1

A SPECIAL KIND OF COURAGE

'Today, we need a special kind of courage ... a kind which makes us stand up for everything that we know is right, everything that is true and honest.'

1957

Many grave problems and difficulties confront us all, but with a new faith in the old and splendid beliefs given us by our forebears, and the strength to venture beyond the safeties of the past, I know we shall be worthy of our duty.

Above all, we must keep alive that courageous spirit of adventure that is the finest quality of youth; and, by youth, I do not just mean those who are young in years; I mean too all those who are young in heart, no matter how old they may be.

1952

In the turbulence of this anxious and active world,
many people are leading uneventful, lonely lives.
To them, dreariness, not disaster, is the enemy.

They seldom realise that on their steadfastness,
on their ability to withstand the fatigue of dull,
repetitive work and on their courage in meeting
constant small adversities, depend in great measure
the happiness and prosperity of the community
as a whole.

1954

Today, we need a special kind of courage, not the kind needed in battle but a kind which makes us stand up for everything that we know is right, everything that is true and honest. We need the kind of courage that can withstand the subtle corruption of the cynics so that we can show the world that we are not afraid of the future.

It has always been easy to hate and destroy. To build and to cherish is much more difficult.

1957

We face grave problems in the life of our country, but our predecessors, and many alive today, have faced far greater difficulties, both in peace and war, and have overcome them by courage and calm determination. They never lost hope and they never lacked confidence in themselves or in their children.

1980

There are, of course, many aspects of courage.

There is the physical courage shown in war. Chesterton described it as 'almost a contradiction in terms ... a strong desire to live taking the form of a readiness to die'.[1] It is sobering and inspiring to remember what people will do for an ideal in which they believe.

Bravery of this kind is shown in peace as well as in war. The armed forces and the police are showing it every day. So are the fire services, ambulance drivers, members of the public and even children – and the courage of the bomb disposal experts fills us with awe. All around us, we see these acts of selflessness, people putting the life of someone else before their own.

1981

I have spoken of courage in its different forms and of the effect a display of courage can have on the world in which we live. Ultimately, however, we accept in our hearts that most important of all is moral courage.

As human beings, we generally know what is right, and how we should act and speak. But we are also very aware of how difficult it is to have the courage of our convictions. Our Christian faith helps us to sustain those convictions. Christ not only revealed to us the truth in his teachings. He lived by what he believed and gave us the strength to try to do the same – and, finally, on the cross, he showed the supreme example of physical and moral courage.

1981

For many, the future is a source of excitement, hope and challenge. For others, however, the future is a cause of understandable anxiety. There are many, for example, of my age or amongst the more vulnerable in society who worry that they will be left behind. The sheer rate of change seems to be sweeping away so much that is familiar and comforting.

But I do not think that we should be over-anxious. We can make sense of the future – if we understand the lessons of the past. Winston Churchill, my first prime minister, said that 'the further backward you look, the further forward you can see.'[2]

1999

When life seems hard, the courageous do not lie down and accept defeat; instead, they are all the more determined to struggle for a better future.

2008

It's in hardship that we often find strength from our families; it's in adversity that new friendships are sometimes formed; and it's in a crisis that communities break down barriers and bind together to help one another.

Families, friends and communities often find a source of courage rising up from within. Indeed, sadly, it seems that it is tragedy that often draws out the most and the best from the human spirit.

2011

When people face a challenge, they sometimes talk about taking a deep breath to find courage or strength. In fact, the word 'inspire' literally means 'to breathe in'. But even with the inspiration of others, it's understandable that we sometimes think the world's problems are so big that we can do little to help. On our own, we cannot end wars or wipe out injustice, but the cumulative impact of thousands of small acts of goodness can be bigger than we imagine.

2016

PART 2

PEOPLE MATTER

'Humanity has many blemishes, but deep down in every soul there is a store of goodwill waiting to be called upon.'

1966

All the great works of charity have always been
inspired by a flame of compassion which has
burnt brightly in the hearts of men and women.
Humanity has many blemishes, but deep down in
every soul there is a store of goodwill waiting to
be called upon.

1966

Christ taught love and charity, and that we should show humanity and compassion, at all times and in all situations.

A lack of humanity and compassion can be very destructive – how easily this causes divisions within nations and between nations. We should remember, instead, how much we have in common and resolve to give expression to the best of our human qualities.

1973

People in a crowd may seem oblivious of each other. Yet if you look at your neighbours, you will see other people with worries and difficulties probably greater than your own. It is time to recognise that, in the end, we all depend upon each other and that we are therefore responsible for each other.

1974

Christmas is a festival which brings us together in small groups, a family group if we are lucky. Today, we are not just nameless people in a crowd. We meet as friends who are glad to be together and who care about one another's happiness.

Nowadays, this is a precious experience. So much of the time we feel that our lives are dominated by great impersonal forces beyond our control; the scale of things and organisations seems to get bigger and more inhuman.

Then Christmas comes, and once again we are reminded that people matter, and it is our relationship with one another that is most important.

1975

The future is not only about new gadgets, modern technology or the latest fashion, important as these may be. At the centre of our lives – today and tomorrow – must be the message of caring for others, the message at the heart of Christianity and of all the great religions.

This message – love your neighbour as yourself – may be over two thousand years old. But it is as relevant today as it ever was.

1999

Even in our very material age, the impact of Christ's
life is all around us. If you want to see an expression
of Christian faith you have only to look at our
awe-inspiring cathedrals and abbeys, listen to their
music, or look at their stained-glass windows, their
books and their pictures. But the true measure
of Christ's influence is not only in the lives of the
saints but also in the good works quietly done by
millions of men and women day in and day out
throughout the centuries.

2000

Whether we believe in God or not, I think most of us have a sense of the spiritual, that recognition of a deeper meaning and purpose in our lives, and I believe that this sense flourishes despite the pressures of our world.

To many of us, our beliefs are of fundamental importance. For me, the teachings of Christ and my own personal accountability before God provide a framework in which I try to lead my life.

I believe that the Christian message, in the words of a familiar blessing, remains profoundly important to us all:

'Go forth into the world in peace, be of good courage, hold fast that which is good, render to no man evil for evil, strengthen the faint-hearted, support the weak, help the afflicted, honour all men.'[3]

It is a simple message of compassion and yet as powerful as ever today, two thousand years after Christ's birth.

2000

Throughout his ministry, Jesus of Nazareth reached
out and made friends with people whom others
ignored or despised. It was in this way that he
proclaimed his belief that, in the end, we are all
brothers and sisters in one human family.

The Christmas story also draws attention to all
those people who are on the edge of society –
people who feel cut off and disadvantaged; people
who, for one reason or another, are not able to
enjoy the full benefits of living in a civilised and
law-abiding community.

2007

Over the years, those who have seemed to me to be the most happy, contented and fulfilled have always been the people who have lived the most outgoing and unselfish lives; the kind of people who are generous with their talents or their time. They tend to have some sense that life itself is full of blessings and is a precious gift for which we should be thankful.

2008

Remarkably, a year that has necessarily kept people apart has, in many ways, brought us closer. In the United Kingdom and around the world, people have risen magnificently to the challenges of the year, and I am so proud and moved by this quiet, indomitable spirit.

We continue to be inspired by the kindness of strangers and draw comfort that – even on the darkest nights – there is hope in the new dawn.

Jesus touched on this with the parable of the Good Samaritan. The man who is robbed and left at the roadside is saved by someone who did not share his religion or culture. This wonderful story of kindness is still as relevant today. Good Samaritans have emerged across society showing care and respect for all, regardless of gender, race or background, reminding us that each one of us is special and equal in the eyes of God.

2020

PART 3

FORGIVE AND RESPECT

'A civilised and peaceful existence is only possible when people make the effort to understand one another.'

1972

Deep and acute differences, involving both intellect
and emotion, are bound to arise between members
of a family and also between friend and friend,
and there is neither virtue nor value in pretending
that they do not. In all such differences, however,
there comes a moment when, for the sake of
ultimate harmony, the healing power of tolerance,
comradeship and love must be allowed to play
its part.

I speak of a tolerance that is not indifference, but
is rather a willingness to recognise the possibility
of right in others; of a comradeship that is not
just a sentimental memory of good days past, but
the certainty that the tried and staunch friends of
yesterday are still in truth the same people today;
of a love that can rise above anger and is ready
to forgive.

1956

We know only too well that a selfish insistence upon our rights and our own point of view leads to disaster. We all ought to know by now that a civilised and peaceful existence is only possible when people make the effort to understand one another.

1972

It is easy enough to see where reconciliation
is needed and where it would heal and purify,
obviously in national and international affairs, but
also in homes and families. It is not something that
is easy to achieve. But things that are worthwhile
seldom are.

Remember that good spreads outwards and
every little does help. Mighty things from small
beginnings grow. If there is reconciliation – if we
can get the climate right – the good effects will
flow much more quickly than most people would
believe possible.

Those who know the desert know also how quickly
it can flower when the rains come. When the
conflict stops, peace can blossom just as quickly.

1976

There are any number of reasons to find fault with each other, with our governments and with other countries. But let us not take ourselves too seriously. None of us has a monopoly of wisdom and we must always be ready to listen and respect other points of view.

1991

Religion and culture are much in the news these days, usually as sources of difference and conflict, rather than for bringing people together. But the irony is that every religion has something to say about tolerance and respecting others.

For me as a Christian, one of the most important of these teachings is contained in the parable of the Good Samaritan, when Jesus answers the question, 'Who is my neighbour?' It is a timeless story of a victim of a mugging who was ignored by his own countrymen but helped by a foreigner – and a despised foreigner at that.

The implication drawn by Jesus is clear. Everyone is our neighbour, no matter what race, creed or colour. The need to look after a fellow human being is far more important than any cultural or religious differences.

2004

Most of us have learned to acknowledge and respect the ways of other cultures and religions, but what matters even more is the way in which those from different backgrounds behave towards each other in everyday life.

They all need to be reassured that there is so much to be gained by reaching out to others; that diversity is indeed a strength and not a threat.

2004

Although we are capable of great acts of kindness, history teaches us that we sometimes need saving from ourselves – from our recklessness or our greed. God sent into the world a unique person – neither a philosopher nor a general (important though they are) – but a Saviour, with the power to forgive.

Forgiveness lies at the heart of the Christian faith. It can heal broken families, it can restore friendships and it can reconcile divided communities. It is in forgiveness that we feel the power of God's love.

2011

For me, the life of Jesus Christ, the Prince of
Peace, is an inspiration and an anchor in my life.
A role model of reconciliation and forgiveness, he
stretched out his hands in love, acceptance and
healing. Christ's example has taught me to seek
to respect and value all people of whatever faith
or none.

2014

In 1914, many people thought the war would be over by Christmas, but sadly by then the trenches were dug and the future shape of the war in Europe was set. But, as we know, something remarkable did happen that Christmas. Without any instruction or command, the shooting stopped and German and British soldiers met in No Man's Land. Photographs were taken and gifts exchanged. It was a Christmas truce.

Sometimes it seems that reconciliation stands little chance in the face of war and discord. But, as the Christmas truce a century ago reminds us, peace and goodwill have lasting power in the hearts of men and women.

2014

Since the end of the Second World War, many
charities, groups and organisations have worked
to promote peace and unity around the world,
bringing together those who have been on opposing
sides. By being willing to put past differences
behind us and move forward together, we honour
the freedom and democracy once won for us at so
great a cost.

It is often the small steps, not the giant leaps, that
bring about the most lasting change.

2019

PART 4

WITH LOVE IN
OUR HEARTS

'There are many serious and threatening problems in
the world but they will never be solved until there is
peace in our homes and love in our hearts.'

1986

Scientists talk of 'chain reaction' – of power releasing yet more power. This principle must be most true when it is applied to the greatest power of all: the power of love.

1955

Christ commanded us to love our neighbours as we love ourselves, but what exactly is meant by 'loving ourselves'? I believe it means trying to make the most of the abilities we have been given; it means caring for our talents.

It is a matter of making the best of ourselves, not just doing the best for ourselves.

1975

When, as the Bible says, Christ grew in wisdom and understanding, he began his task of explaining and teaching just what it is that God wants from us. The two lessons that he had for us, which he underlined in everything he said and did, are the messages of God's love and how essential it is that we, too, should love other people.

There are many serious and threatening problems in the world but they will never be solved until there is peace in our homes and love in our hearts.

1986

Men and women have shown themselves to be very clever at inventing things, right back to the time when they found out how much easier it was to move things about on wheels, up to the present time when rockets and computers make it possible for people to travel away from our world into the mystery of space.

But these technical skills are not enough by themselves. They can only come to the rescue of the planet if we also learn to live by the golden rule which Jesus Christ taught us: 'Love your neighbour as yourself.'

1989

St Paul spoke of the first Christmas as the kindness of God dawning upon the world. The world needs that kindness now more than ever – the kindness and consideration for others that disarms malice and allows us to get on with one another with respect and affection.

Christmas reassures us that God is with us today. But, as I have discovered for myself, he is always present in the kindness shown by our neighbours and the love of our friends and family.

1997

We all need to get the balance right between action and reflection. With so many distractions, it is easy to forget to pause and take stock. Be it through contemplation, prayer or even keeping a diary, many have found the practice of quiet personal reflection surprisingly rewarding, even discovering greater spiritual depth to their lives.

Reflection can take many forms. For Christians, as for all people of faith, reflection, meditation and prayer help us to renew ourselves in God's love, as we strive daily to become better people. The Christmas message shows us that this love is for everyone. There is no one beyond its reach.

2013

For every poppy a life; and a reminder of the grief
of loved ones left behind.

2014

Despite being displaced and persecuted throughout his short life, Christ's unchanging message was not one of revenge or violence but simply that we should love one another. Although it is not an easy message to follow, we shouldn't be discouraged; rather, it inspires us to try harder: to be thankful for the people who bring love and happiness into our own lives, and to look for ways of spreading that love to others, whenever and wherever we can.

2015

Jesus Christ lived obscurely for most of his life, and never travelled far. He was maligned and rejected by many, though he had done no wrong. And yet, billions of people now follow his teaching and find in him the guiding light for their lives. I am one of them because Christ's example helps me see the value of doing small things with great love, whoever does them and whatever they themselves believe.

2016

We think of our homes as places of warmth, familiarity and love; of shared stories and memories, which is perhaps why at this time of year so many return to where they grew up. There is a timeless simplicity to the pull of home.

Today, we celebrate Christmas, which itself is sometimes described as a festival of the home. Families travel long distances to be together. Volunteers and charities, as well as many churches, arrange meals for the homeless and those who would otherwise be alone on Christmas Day. We remember the birth of Jesus Christ whose only sanctuary was a stable in Bethlehem. He knew rejection, hardship and persecution; and yet it is Jesus Christ's generous love and example which has inspired me through good times and bad.

2017

PART 5

THE WISDOM
OF CHILDREN

'No age group has a monopoly of wisdom, and indeed
I think the young can sometimes be wiser than us.'

1998

Our children will be living in a world which our work and deeds have shaped for them. We leave them with a set of values which they take from our lives and from our example. The decisions they take and the sort of world they pass on to their children could be just as much affected by those values as by all the technological wonders of the age.

1971

We must not forget that every generation has to face the problems of childhood and the stresses of growing up, and, in due course, the responsibilities of parents and adults.

Schools, charities and voluntary organisations and institutions can do a great deal to help; but, in the end, each one of us has a primary and personal responsibility for our own children, for children entrusted to our care and for all the children in our communities.

1979

For parents and grandparents, a birth is a time for
reflection on what the future holds for the baby and
how they can best ensure its safety and happiness.
To do that, I believe we must be prepared to learn
as much from them as they do from us. We could
use some of that sturdy confidence and devastating
honesty with which children rescue us from self-
doubts and self-delusions. We could borrow that
unstinting trust of the child in its parents for our
dealings with each other.

1984

Above all, we must retain the child's readiness to forgive, with which we are all born and which it is all too easy to lose as we grow older. Without it, divisions between families, communities and nations remain unbridgeable. We owe it to our children and grandchildren to live up to the standards of behaviour and tolerance which we are so eager to teach them.

1984

Christmas commemorates the birth of a child, who was born to ordinary people, and who grew up very simply in his own small home town. The infant Jesus was fortunate in one very important respect. His parents were loving and considerate. They did their utmost to protect him from harm. They left their own home and became refugees to save him from King Herod, and they brought him up according to the traditions of their faith.

It is no easy task to care for and bring up children, whatever your circumstances. But we could all help by letting the spirit of Christmas fill our homes with love and care, and by heeding our Lord's injunction to treat others as you would like them to treat you.

1986

It is not always easy for those in their teens or twenties to believe that someone of my age – of the older generation – might have something useful to say to them. But with age does come experience, and that can be a virtue if it is sensibly used. Though we each lead different lives, the experience of growing older, and the joys and emotions which it brings, are familiar to us all.

As a daughter, a mother and a grandmother, I often find myself seeking advice, or being asked for it, in all three capacities. No age group has a monopoly of wisdom, and indeed I think the young can sometimes be wiser than us. But the older I get, the more conscious I become of the difficulties young people have to face as they learn to live in the modern world.

We parents and grandparents must learn to trust our children and grandchildren as they seize their opportunities, but we can, at the same time, caution and comfort if things go wrong, or guide and explain if we are needed.

1998

I particularly enjoyed a story I heard the other day about an overseas visitor to Britain who said the best part of his visit had been travelling from Heathrow into Central London on the Tube. His British friends were, as you can imagine, somewhat surprised. 'What do you mean?' they asked.

Because, he replied, I boarded the train just as the schools were coming out. At each stop, children were getting on and off – they were of every ethnic and religious background, some with scarves or turbans, some talking quietly, others playing and occasionally misbehaving together – completely at ease and trusting one another. How lucky you are, said the visitor, to live in a country where your children can grow up this way.

I hope they will be allowed to enjoy this happy companionship for the rest of their lives.

2004

The wisdom and experience of the great religions point to the need to nurture and guide the young, and to encourage respect for the elderly. Christ himself told his disciples to let the children come to him, and St Paul reminded parents to be gentle with their children, and children to appreciate their parents.

The scriptures and traditions of the other faiths enshrine the same fundamental guidance. It is very easy to concentrate on the differences between the religious faiths and to forget what they have in common. People of different faiths are bound together by the need to help the younger generation to become considerate and active citizens.

2006

I have lived long enough to know that things never remain quite the same for very long. One of the things that has not changed all that much for me is the celebration of Christmas. It remains a time when I try to put aside the anxieties of the moment and remember that Christ was born to bring peace and tolerance to a troubled world.

The birth of Jesus naturally turns our thoughts to all newborn children and what the future holds for them. For Christians, Christmas marks the birth of our Saviour, but it is also a wonderful occasion to bring the generations together in a shared festival of peace, tolerance and goodwill.

2006

I am sure someone somewhere today will remark
that Christmas is a time for children. It's an
engaging truth, but only half the story. Perhaps it's
truer to say that Christmas can speak to the child
within us all. Adults, when weighed down with
worries, sometimes fail to see the joy in simple
things, where children do not.

And for me and my family, even with one familiar
laugh missing this year, there will be joy in
Christmas, as we have the chance to reminisce, and
see anew the wonder of the festive season through
the eyes of our young children. They teach us all
a lesson – just as the Christmas story does – that
in the birth of a child, there is a new dawn with
endless potential.

2021

PART 6

STRONGER
TOGETHER

'We all enjoy moments of great happiness and suffer
times of profound sadness; the happiness is heightened,
the sadness softened when it is shared.'

2001

We are amazed by the spectacular discoveries in scientific knowledge, which should bring comfort and leisure to millions. We do not always reflect that these things also have rested to some extent on the faithful toil and devotion to duty of the great bulk of ordinary citizens. The upward course of a nation's history is due, in the long run, to the soundness of heart of its average men and women.

1954

We are all different, but each of us has our own best to offer. The responsibility for the way we live life, with all its challenges, sadness and joy, is ours alone. If we do this well, it will also be good for our neighbours.

If you throw a stone into a pool, the ripples go on spreading outwards. A big stone can cause waves, but even the smallest pebble changes the whole pattern of the water. Our daily actions are like those ripples – each one makes a difference, even the smallest.

1975

We have the means of sending and receiving messages, but we still have difficulty in finding the right messages to send. We can ignore the messages we don't like to hear and we can talk in riddles and listen without trying to comprehend. Perhaps even more serious is the risk that mastery of technology may blind us to the more fundamental needs of people. Electronics cannot create comradeship; computers cannot generate compassion; satellites cannot transmit tolerance.

It is not how we communicate but what we communicate with each other that really matters.

1983

Many of you will have heard of the greenhouse effect, and perhaps you've heard too about even more urgent problems caused by the pollution of our rivers and seas and the cutting down of the great forests. These problems make neighbourly cooperation throughout the world a pressing necessity.

You've all seen pictures of the Earth taken from space. Unlike all the other planets in the solar system, Earth shimmers green and blue in the sunlight and looks a very pleasant place to live. These pictures should remind us that the future of all life on Earth depends on how we behave towards one another, and how we treat the plants and the animals that share our world with us.

1989

65

There are all sorts of elements to a free society, but
I believe that among the most important is the
willingness of ordinary men and women to play
a part in the life of their community, rather than
confining themselves to their own narrow interests.

1991

Being united – that is, feeling a unity of purpose – is the glue that bonds together the members of a family, a country, a Commonwealth. Without it, the parts are only fragments of a whole; with it, we can be much more than the sum of those fragments.

1997

I believe that strong and open communities matter in good times as well as bad. Certainly, they provide a way of helping one another. Communities also give us an important sense of belonging, which is a compelling need in all of us. We all enjoy moments of great happiness and suffer times of profound sadness; the happiness is heightened, the sadness softened when it is shared.

2001

A sense of belonging to a group, which has
in common the desire for a fair and ordered
society, helps to overcome differences and
misunderstanding by reducing prejudice,
ignorance and fear.

2001

In the parks of towns and cities, and on village greens up and down the country, countless thousands of people every week give up their time to participate in sport and exercise of all sorts, or simply encourage others to do so. These kinds of activity are common throughout the world and play a part in providing a different perspective on life.

Apart from developing physical fitness, sport and games can also teach vital social skills. None can be enjoyed without abiding by the rules, and no team can hope to succeed without cooperation between the players. This sort of positive team spirit can benefit communities, companies and enterprises of all kinds.

2010

Nothing is more satisfying than the feeling of
belonging to a group who are dedicated to helping
each other.

2010

PART 7

HOPE FOR TOMORROW

'It is through the lens of history that we should view the conflicts of today, and so give us hope for tomorrow.'

2011

'Peace on Earth' – we may not have it at the moment, we may never have it completely, but we will certainly achieve nothing unless we go on trying to remove the causes of conflict between peoples and nations.

'Goodwill toward men' is not a hollow phrase. Goodwill exists, and when there is an opportunity to show it in practical form, we know what wonderful things it can achieve.

1965

We must not let the difficulties of the present or the uncertainties of the future cause us to lose faith. You remember the saying, 'The optimist proclaims that we live in the best of all possible worlds, and the pessimist fears that this is true.'[4] It is far from easy to be cheerful and constructive when things around us suggest the opposite; but to give up the effort would mean, as it were, to switch off hope for a better tomorrow.

Even if the problems seem overwhelming, there is always room for optimism. Every problem presents us with the opportunity both to find an answer for ourselves and to help others.

1978

We know that the world can never be free from conflict and pain, but Christmas draws our attention to all that is hopeful and good in this changing world; it speaks of values and qualities that are true and permanent, and it reminds us that the world we would like to see can only come from the goodness of the heart.

1980

What is it that makes people turn from violence,
and try to bring peace to their community?
Most of all, I believe, it is their determination to
bring reality to their hopes of a better world for
their children.

1994

In difficult times, it is tempting for all of us, especially those who suffer, to look back and say, 'If only ...' But to look back in that way is to look down a blind alley. Better to look forward and say, 'If only ...'

If only we can live up to the example of the child who was born at Christmas with a love that came to embrace the whole world. If only we can let him recapture for us that time when we faced the future with childhood's unbounded faith.

1996

So many of us, whatever our religion, need our faith more than ever to sustain and guide us. Every one of us needs to believe in the value of all that is good and honest; we need to let this belief drive and influence our actions.

All the major faiths tell us to give support and hope to others in distress.

2001

Each day is a new beginning; I know that the only way to live my life is to try to do what is right, to take the long view, to give of my best in all that the day brings, and to put my trust in God.

2002

We need to realise that peaceful and steady progress in our society of differing cultures and heritage can be threatened at any moment by the actions of extremists at home or by events abroad. We can certainly never be complacent.

But there is every reason to be hopeful about the future. I certainly recognise that much has been achieved in my lifetime. I believe tolerance and fair play remain strong British values and we have so much to build on for the future.

2004

It is through the lens of history that we should view the conflicts of today, and so give us hope for tomorrow.

2011

Some cultures believe a long life brings wisdom. I'd like to think so. Perhaps part of that wisdom is to recognise some of life's baffling paradoxes, such as the way human beings have a huge propensity for good, and yet a capacity for evil. Even the power of faith, which frequently inspires great generosity and self-sacrifice, can fall victim to tribalism. But through the many changes I have seen over the years, faith, family and friendship have been not only a constant for me but a source of personal comfort and reassurance.

2018

Notes

1 G. K. Chesterton, 'Paradoxes of Christianity', from *Orthodoxy* (1908).

2 Paraphrase of Winston Churchill, 'The longer you can look back, the farther you can look forward', Royal College of Physicians, London, 2 March 1944.

3 Adapted from The Book of Common Prayer (1928). Extracts from The Book of Common Prayer, the rights in which are vested in the Crown, are reproduced by permission of the Crown's Patentee, Cambridge University Press.

4 James Branch Cabell, *The Silver Stallion* (1926).

Sources and
acknowledgements

Photo © Philip Mould Ltd, London / © Estate of Norman Hepple. All rights reserved 2024 / Bridgeman Images.

36   Michael Leonard (1933–2023), *Queen Elizabeth II* (1985–86).
© Estate of Michael Leonard.

48   Susan Ryder (b. 1944), *Her Majesty the Queen Elizabeth II* (1996).
© Susan Ryder. All rights reserved 2024 / Bridgeman Images.

60   Chinwe Chukwuogo-Roy (1952–2012), *Portrait of Elizabeth II* (2002).
Nils Jorgensen / Shutterstock. © Chinwe Chukwuogo-Roy. All rights reserved, DACS 2024.

72   Isobel Peachey, *Queen Elizabeth II* (2010).
© Isobel Peachey. Collection of Cunard on board the Queen Elizabeth.

Majesty

Read on for extracts from *Majesty: Reflections on the life of Christ with Her Majesty Queen Elizabeth II* by Richard Harries

Reflections on the Life of Christ
with Queen Elizabeth II

RICHARD HARRIES

See https://spckpublishing.co.uk/majesty-6

1
LIGHT OF THE WORLD

'St Paul spoke of the first Christmas as the
kindness of God dawning upon the world. The
world needs that kindness now more than ever.'

The Queen's Christmas broadcast, 1997

DETAIL FROM
**THE ADORATION OF
THE SHEPHERDS**
Jacopo Bassano (1510–92)
King's drawing room,
Kensington Palace

Extracts from *Majesty* by Richard Harries

The annunciation

In the sixth month, the angel Gabriel was sent by God to a town in Galilee called Nazareth, to a virgin engaged to a man whose name was Joseph, of the house of David. The virgin's name was Mary. And he came to her and said, 'Greetings, favoured one! The Lord is with you.' But she was much perplexed by his words and pondered what sort of greeting this might be. The angel said to her, 'Do not be afraid, Mary, for you have found favour with God. And now, you will conceive in your womb and bear a son, and you will name him Jesus. He will be great, and will be called the Son of the Most High, and the Lord God will give to him the throne of his ancestor David. He will reign over the house of Jacob for ever, and of his kingdom there will be no end.' Mary said to the angel, 'How can this be, since I am a virgin?' The angel said to her, 'The Holy Spirit will come upon you, and the power of the Most High will overshadow you; therefore the child to be born will be holy; he will be called Son of God. And now, your relative Elizabeth in her old age has also conceived a son; and this is the sixth month for her who was said to be barren. For nothing will be impossible with God.' Then Mary said, 'Here am I, the servant of the Lord; let it be with me according to your word.' Then the angel departed from her.

From the Gospel of Luke, chapter 1

THE ANNUNCIATION
Carlo Maratti (1625–1713)
Queen's private chapel,
Hampton Court Palace

The annunciation was depicted in the fifth century, in a mosaic, and may even have been painted earlier than this in the catacombs. By the time of Fra Angelico in the fifteenth century it was a familiar scene in art. Fra Angelico was a monk and his version exudes quiet prayerfulness.

The version here by Maratti could not be more different. It is dramatic, even theatrical. The angel Gabriel, a towering figure with right arm raised, appears overpowering. Angels and putti are all around but almost pushed aside. Mary to the left looks up at him with a sense of surprise and questioning. Gabriel carries a white lily, the traditional symbol of Mary, who wears blue, her traditional colour, and is shown reading a book. It is open at Isaiah 7.14–16 (AV): 'Therefore the Lord himself shall give you a sign; Behold, a virgin shall conceive, and bear a son, and shall call his name Immanuel.'

The Holy Spirit, symbolized as a dove, overshadows Mary. The face of God the Father in outline looms above – which is incorrect theologically. According to Christian theology, God in himself is totally unknown and incomprehensible so should not be depicted in art. But God has made himself known in a way that we humans can understand, in Jesus, the Word made flesh. It is his life that justifies Christian art.

Maratti's version reflects two main influences, one religious and the other artistic. In response to the Protestant Reformation, the Roman Catholic Church made strenuous attempts to reform its life, known as the Counter-Reformation.

Religious orders were founded and missionaries went all over the world, inspired with a new zeal. Their preaching was dramatic, and they used theatre to get their message across. Although Maratti stood in the Classical tradition of Raphael, he was influenced by the much more flamboyant Baroque art. It is an art designed to depict, and get the viewer to share, strong emotions. So one of its features is light and glory, very much to the fore here with light breaking through the clouds and lighting up the darkness below. And it is right for it to be dramatic, for what could be more astounding than the Eternal Word taking form as a human person? What more glorious than Eternal Love sharing human vulnerability?

The angel Gabriel, a towering figure with
right arm raised, appears overpowering.

5
EASTER GLORY

'The simple facts of Jesus' life give us little
clue as to the influence he was to have on the
world. His ministry only lasted a few years
and he himself never wrote anything down. In
his early thirties he was arrested, tortured and
crucified with two criminals. His death might
have been the end of the story, but then came
the resurrection and with it the foundation of
the Christian faith.'

The Queen's Christmas broadcast, 2000

DETAIL FROM
THE LIGHT OF THE WORLD
Holman Hunt (1827–1910)
Keble College, Oxford

Extracts from *Majesty* by Richard Harries

The disciple who doubted

DOUBTING THOMAS
Early eleventh-century mosaic
Osios Loukas, Greece

When it was evening on that day, the first day of
the week, and the doors of the house where the
disciples had met were locked for fear of the Jews,
Jesus came and stood among them and said, 'Peace
be with you.' After he said this, he showed them
his hands and his side. Then the disciples rejoiced
when they saw the Lord. Jesus said to them again,
'Peace be with you. As the Father has sent me, so I
send you.' When he had said this, he breathed on
them and said to them, 'Receive the Holy Spirit. If
you forgive the sins of any, they are forgiven them;
if you retain the sins of any, they are retained.'

But Thomas (who was called the Twin), one of
the twelve, was not with them when Jesus came.
So the other disciples told him, 'We have seen the
Lord.' But he said to them, 'Unless I see the mark
of the nails in his hands, and put my finger in the
mark of the nails and my hand in his side, I will
not believe.'

A week later his disciples were again in the house,
and Thomas was with them. Although the doors
were shut, Jesus came and stood among them and
said, 'Peace be with you.' Then he said to Thomas,
'Put your finger here and see my hands. Reach out
your hand and put it in my side. Do not doubt but
believe.' Thomas answered him, 'My Lord and my
God!' Jesus said to him, 'Have you believed because
you have seen me? Blessed are those who have not
seen and yet have come to believe.'

From the Gospel of John, chapter 20

Extracts from *Majesty* by Richard Harries

The small monastery of Osios Loukas, on the north of the Gulf of Corinth in Greece, is a gem. Unassuming from the outside, it contains superb mosaics from a fine period of Byzantine art. The Gospel tells us that Thomas was not present at the first appearance of the risen Christ to the disciples and doubted its truth. Here Christ appears again and offers Thomas a chance to see the wounds. He holds his hand up and pulls aside the robe covering his side. Thomas (his face badly damaged) holds out his hand and points his finger at the side of Christ, though not in the dramatic manner later depicted by Caravaggio. The other ten Apostles look on, Judas no longer being of their number.

Christ in the centre appears against a background which is both a door and a sarcophagus. The words above the door read in translation, 'The doors being shut', from John chapter 20. The door is the shut door which cannot keep Christ out, the grave which cannot hold him, and the entry into eternal life.

In April 2021, when the world was struck down by the Covid-19 virus, Her Majesty the Queen reflected:

'The discovery of the risen Christ on the first Easter Day gave his followers new hope and fresh purpose, and we can all take heart from this. We know that Coronavirus will not overcome us. As dark as death can be – particularly for those suffering with grief – light and life are greater. May the living flame of the Easter hope be a steady guide as we face the future.'